Slay the
E-mail Monster

96 Easy Ways to Dramatically
Increase Productivity

Lynn Coffman & Michael Valentine

ISBN: 1451550030
ISBN-13: 9781451550030

Table of Contents

Kudos
(for the cover)

"…Your workshop was one of the best I've ever attended, and I've attended many!"

Dr. John Forde, Head Department of Communications, Miss State Univ.

"I wanted to thank you for bringing in the consultants who talked about 'Slaying the E-mail Monster' (Muda). It's completely changed my e-mail habits - I spend significantly less time wading through e-mail"

Ben Johnson, Web Marketing Manager, UC San Diego Extension

"Thanks for your insights. I have regained 6 to 8 hours of my work week that I was wasting with e-mails, meetings, and searching for information. Now everything is organized, in its place and I leave every day with zero items in my e-mail inbox. More important, I am using these reclaimed hours to do productive work that really matters to my organization.

I've accomplished more important items this month than I did in the previous three months combined."

Henry DeVries, Assistant Dean, UC San Diego Extension

"Of all the sessions I attended at the 2009 PRSA International Conference in San Diego last week, the one that may end up having the most profound impact on the way I work was the final session. ...The title was 'Dramatically Increase Productivity by Slaying the E-mail Monster', by Michael Valentine and Lynn Coffman, the principals of Coffman Valentine & Associates."

Dan Keeney, DPK Public Relations

Introduction: Kill the Muda

Before you slay your e-mail monster, you should know that it has a name: muda.

The e-mail monster is a real problem. Talk to most people in corporations today and you will hear a common recurring theme, "I am swamped with e-mail!" E-mail overload is considered an inescapable fact in this information, wireless and digital age. Schedules are disrupted. Priorities are changed. The volume of e-mail grows and the stress increases exponentially. In fact workers have come to believe that this is a normal part of work. If you ask office workers what they do, most will begin by saying that they spend too much time processing e-mail.

When e-mail communications on our desktop computers revolutionized the workplace in the mid 1990s, the monster was not large at first; but it has grown over time. When laptop computers gained more widespread use, these machines allowed us to transport our e-mail portal to the world, and the e-mail monster grew even larger. Now nearly everyone has true mobility with the remarkable new business PDA/Smartphone tools like a Pocket PC, the Blackberry, and the iPhone. These advances in technology offer both good news and bad news.

The good news is that they increase personal productivity by making people available 24/7. The bad news is that they increase personal stress by making people available 24/7. They have become the new business narcotic, every bit as addictive as crack cocaine. These devices weren't just given the nickname Crackberry, they earned it.

This book is for knowledge workers, those employees who deal in information, ideas, and expertise. With knowledge workers, the emphasis is on problem solving, creativity and innovation. According to management guru Peter Drucker, the man who coined the term in 1959, in the new computerized economy every employee is becoming a knowledge worker.

The result of the e-mail and PDA dynamics is that knowledge workers have become swamped with e-mail all the time, no matter where they are or what they are doing. If this situation really contributed to increased production of value work, it would at least offer some redemption. The truth is that the promised productivity increase is not being fully realized. In fact, there is an increasing level of burn-out in knowledge workers.

In our years coaching knowledge workers at all levels, one thing has become clear. The need to exploit the promised benefits of the technology has caused workers to forget the process altogether. The process is not e-mail; it is *business communication.*

When We Met Muda

In our productivity coaching at Toyota Motor Sales, U.S.A., Inc., we were asked to apply the principles of Lean to the automaker's office workers, including the concept of waste reduction as a means of increasing profitability. We learned the Japanese have a word for any activity that is wasteful and doesn't add value or is unproductive: muda.

The mishandling of e-mail was one of the biggest and most frustrating knowledge worker mudas we discovered. Two things were happening. The productivity losses from e-mail were relentlessly stealing small chunks of time that added up to hours per week. Secondly, many knowledge workers were making up for the productivity losses in ways that the manufacturing workers could not: the knowledge workers were doing it on their own time by handling e-mails at night and on weekends. Worker burn out is an inevitable result. The muda is killing us.

To date, Lean has succeeded to a much greater degree in manufacturing than in service environments. It is easier for people to see the application of Lean to manufacturing work as it is tangible and linear. Most knowledge work is intangible and non linear. But the principles still apply.

Knowledge workers know that their work activities are in a knot. They don't see their work as a series of interrelated process streams. During our coaching we identify and unravel the strands, and reintegrate them to show that there is a process and a better way to work efficiently and effectively.

In order to regain control of e-mail and realize the real productivity increases that the tools promise, we suggest the following first steps:

Realize that e-mail is just a communication channel. It is not a job. If the business message can be effectively communicated with another means, then that may be a better channel. Paper, telephones, meetings, and even drums are also channels and are equally appropriate if used correctly.

Choose the correct channel for the nature of the communication. E-mail may not be the correct channel to announce that there is a fire in the building. Broadcasting on the PA system may not be the right channel to announce that the company is going to begin a blood drive in two months. Inform others how you intend to use and respond to e-mail.

Determine for yourself when and how often to open your mail. Turn off any signal that alerts you to incoming mail. There is always a perceived urgency to those signals that rarely match the importance of the message. Believe it or not, the Blackberry has an off switch.

Open and deal with every e-mail in your inbox. The inbox is not a file cabinet. It is the mailbox to your environment. Once you look at a message, either delete it or move it to where it belongs. You would never stuff your unpaid bills back in your mailbox at home just because you were not ready to pay them. So don't do that in the e-mail inbox. Create a structure to house work in progress.

Take steps to reduce the volume of e-mail that you receive. Inform your people if you don't need to see every FYI. Ask for exception reporting and reduce the business-as-usual messages. Get off distribution lists that are irrelevant to your job. Teach people how you prefer to be communicated with.

Don't over-distribute. Clean up your distribution lists. Don't reply to all. Avoid sending useless FYI e-mail. Always think if you are using the correct channel for your own business communication.

The Payoff

Even though you are a hard working knowledge worker, our research shows that up to eight hours per week is wasted effort. Following the steps in this book can recover those hours and allow you to focus on what we call value work: projects and tasks that matter most to you and your organization's success.

Additionally you will gain the peace of mind that all tasks are under control, you will reduce your stress because you will be less harried, and you will accomplish increased amounts of valued work that results in both a happy boss and happy clients.

When the knight set off on his quest, his goal was not to kill the dragon. His goal was to find the princess. The dragon was one of the obstacles blocking him from reaching his goal. E-mail issues (muda) are obstacles to reaching the goal of getting your work done effectively and efficiently. So the purpose of this book is to help you slay that monster.

Let's begin to kill the muda before the muda kills you.

Part One.
E-mail

1. Reduce Incoming Volume

Take steps to reduce the amount of e-mail you receive. Every little step you take will result in lighter workloads down the road. Less e-mail is more time to be spent doing what really matters.

Unsubscribe to input that is no longer relevant to your work. Get off distribution lists that have no value. Stop receiving reports from your last position. Stop receiving business-as-usual reports and create thresholds for exception reporting.

2. Beware Boomerang E-mail

Send fewer e-mails and you will receive fewer e-mails. Research shows that for every five e-mails you send, you get three in return. That's because 60 percent of e-mails require some sort of response.

To combat the boomerang e-mail effect, first ask yourself: "Do I really need to send this e-mail?" If you eliminate one out of five e-mails you send out, you will cut the number of incoming e-mails by roughly 12 percent. You also will regain the time you would have spent composing and sending those e-mails.

3. Inbox = Mailbox

Treat your e-mail inbox like your mailbox at home.

Think about your mailbox at your home. Every day you empty it and leave it clean. You don't look at the mail and stick it back in the mailbox, do you? What you do is empty your mailbox every time you go to it. You throw away the junk mail right away. Then you gather all the bills and put them in a designated spot so you know where to find them when you are ready to pay them. That is processing your mailbox to empty. As you can see, processing is more than peeking and less than completing the bill paying. The same is true for your inbox.

So why do you let e-mails pile up in your e-mail inbox? If you do, you are not unusual. Most of us were self-taught when it came to using e-mail and we just coped. The goal is to process the inbox to empty and move the work you have to do to another part of the system. You will then be ready to ready to do it when the time comes.

4. Avoid Priority Trap

Processing is not the same as prioritizing. You can't make priority decisions until you have context.

Some time management systems teach you to assign a priority code, such as A, B, C or 1, 2, 3, to all incoming work. Many are tempted to be in a reactive mode and prioritize e-mails as they are received. This is not the way to slay the e-mail monster.

Knowledge work requires focus and concentration. To paraphrase the father of business management, Peter Drucker, "In knowledge work…the task is not given…it has to be determined." The key is being proactive about the knowledge work you do. Often that means buying out the time to really think about what we do that adds the highest value to the organization. Process first, then prioritize.

5. Two-Mınute Rule

**Decide if you can handle an e-mail in two min-
utes or less as you go through your e-mail inbox. If you can, then handle it right then and be
done with it.**

Slaying the e-mail monster is all about workflow process.
You need to get out of the reactive mode and get into the proactive mode. So don't procrastinate and don't prioritize. If you
can handle an e-mail request, do it now and be done with it.

One of the biggest e-mail productivity thieves is the habit
of reading and rereading e-mails. The trick is to read an e-mail
but once and be done with it.

6. Put E-mail In Its Place

The secret to quickly working on your e-mail is deciding what action is required. Start by creating processing folders that are subsets of your e-mail inbox. These processing folders help you quickly determine which actions need to be done when. Star these folders so that the system places them at the top of the folder list.

You remember the adage "A place for everything and everything in its place." This is especially true when it comes to the e-mail workflow process. The processing involves more than checking your e-mail requests but less than completing them. Putting e-mail in its place is the beginning step that lets you be more productive. Creating these processing folders will support handling the flow of e-mail into your work.

7. Create *Action Folder

Put all e-mails that you can't handle in two minutes or less but need to handle today in the *Action Folder. Resist the temptation to drop everything and handle an action item that will take more than two minutes before you finish emptying your inbox.

At the top of the e-mail select "move to folder" and select *Action. The e-mail will move to that folder and your next e-mail will appear.

Yes, something may be urgent. But how do you know if there isn't something more urgent amongst the remaining e-mails? The mantra is "first process, and then prioritize."

The goal with action folder items is to handle them that business day. Of course, that is not always possible. But as you go through the folder you can prioritize the work and decide which needs to be handled first, second and so on. Any e-mail that needs to be done at a future date can be handled by creating a task and assigning a start date.

The *Action folder is added as a sub folder under Inbox:

Calendar
Contacts
Deleted Items
Inbox
   *Action
Junk E-mail
Notes
Outbox

8. Create *Follow Up Folder

Put all e-mails that require no action on your part, but you want to keep on top of, in the *Follow Up folder. At the top of the e-mail select "move to folder" and select *Follow Up. The e-mail will move to that folder and your next e-mail will appear.

What type of e-mails go into the *Follow Up folder? Many issues require that you periodically check in on the status of requests you have made. Sometimes you are monitoring e-mail conversations that you are copied on. These in-limbo issues need a place to reside, and it is not the typical default of letting them collect in the inbox. These are items that you have the responsibility to be sure they happen, but does not require direct action on your part.

Time should be taken on a daily basis to review what is in the *Follow Up folder. On a weekly basis the folder should be purged of any e-mails that are no longer necessary.

Calendar
Contacts
Deleted Items
Inbox
   *Action
   *Follow Up
Junk E-mail
Notes
Outbox

9. Create *Reading Folder

Put all e-mails that you intend to read later at a more convenient time in the *Reading folder. At the top of the e-mail select "move to folder" and select *Reading. The e-mail will move to that folder and your next e-mail will appear.

Many valuable pieces of information come to us through e-mail. While it may be important to read these items, often it is not effective workflow management to stop what you are doing and read a policy memo, association update or e-newsletter. Instead put them in the *Reading folder and schedule a time to get to them.

Often there are chunks of time between projects and meetings that you could use to attack the *Reading folder. A quick scan of the document may tell you if it is something you need to study in depth or something to file away for future reference. Or you might want to download a batch of reading material to peruse while you are on a business trip or waiting for an appointment.

Calendar
Contacts
Deleted Items
Inbox
    *Action
    *Follow Up
    *Reading
Junk E-mail
Notes
Outbox

10. Beginner Step: Old E-mail Folder

Now this is a step for beginners to the Slay the E-mail Monster approach: create one more folder, the Old E-mail folder. As you clean up your inbox for the first time using the slay the e-mail monster system, send all the e-mails that you can't delete or put into the *Action, *Follow Up or *Reading folders into this folder.

We understand completely clearing out the inbox can be a frightening thought for many. What if they need one of those e-mails? As a crawl, walk, run approach to the process, we have created a beginner approach that we often use with the executives we coach.

Beginners can store e-mails that they want to keep in this Old E-mail folder. This is a noticeable improvement to keeping all those old e-mails in your inbox. This will allow you to check back through this group of e-mails as need be. This is only a beginner step. There is a better way.

Calendar
Contacts
Deleted Items
Inbox
    *Action
    *Follow Up
    *Reading
    Old E-mail
Junk E-mail
Notes
Outbox

11. Intermediate Step: E-mail WARP Drive

Now this is a step for those who want to be more organized with their old e-mails: instead of creating an Old E-mail Folder, create WARP Drive folders. WARP stands for Work, Admin, Reference and Personal.

This is an intermediate step because it moves far beyond the catchall concept of an Old E-mail folder. By creating WARP Drive folders you are beginning the process of organizing the workflow. We recommend numbering these folders with 1-4 to allow the system to arrange them in the proper order. Remember the secret of filing is not putting everything away, but being able to readily find work when you need it. Hunting for information is a huge part of the muda that consumes knowledge workers.

This is what the left menu on Outlook will look like when completed:

Calendar
Contacts
Deleted Items
Inbox
    *Action
    *Follow Up
    *Reading
    1 Work
    2 Admin
    3 Reference
    4 Personal
Junk E-mail
Notes
Outbox

12. Create 1Work Folder

Create a folder with the title 1Work Folder. This is a place to put e-mails about projects, clients, external customers, internal customers and cross-functional teams that you are on.

Work is defined as the value you bring to the organization. Another way to think about work is outputs. This is the place to keep e-mails about the outputs you are expected to produce for the organization.

Here is what your folder organization should look like:

Calendar
Contacts
Deleted Items
Inbox
    *Action
    *Follow Up
    *Reading
    1Work
Junk E-mail
Notes
Outbox

13. Create 2Admin Folder

Create a folder with the title 2Admin. (Admin is short for administration.) This is the place to put e-mail about organizational activities that must be done like forms, expense reports, travel and other like matters.

Admin is not the core work we do, but necessary chores to make sure the organization runs. This also can be defined as the non-core job tasks.

Here is what your folder organization should look like:

Calendar
Contacts
Deleted Items
Inbox
    *Action
    *Follow Up
    *Reading
    1Work
    2Admin
Junk E-mail
Notes
Outbox

14. Create 3Reference Folder

Create a folder with the title 3Reference.

This is organizational information you will need to access. Vendor information, policies and procedures, and benefits are all examples of what might be included in the 3Reference folder.

Here is what your folder organization should look like:

Calendar
Contacts
Deleted Items
Inbox
    *Action
    *Follow Up
    *Reading
    1Work
    2Admin
    3Reference
Junk E-mail
Notes
Outbox

15. Create 4Personal Folder

Create a folder with the title 4Personal. This is where to put e-mails about personal interests and activities.

Having a separate work e-mail system and a personal e-mail system is not always practical. So the next best thing is to separate the personal e-mails you need to save from the work e-mails you save. Creating a separate folder also reduces personal muda as you search for necessary personal information.

Some of the items stored in the 4Personal folder include information about family, friends, hobbies, spiritual pursuits, fitness, recreation and health. Please be aware of your organization's policies about the receipt and storage of personal e-mails. Also understand that whatever is stored on organization servers is subject to inspection.

Here is what your folder organization should look like:

Calendar
Contacts
Deleted Items
Inbox
    *Action
    *Follow Up
    *Reading
    1Work
    2Admin
    3Reference
    4Personal
Junk E-mail
Notes
Outbox

16. Continue
Organizing E-mail

If you already have a long string of folders, now is the time to determine if you need any of them. If not, DELETE!

Of course you could have one long list of folders. But much time would be wasted searching the list each time you need information (although a vast improvement again of having everything stay in the inbox). For those folders you need to keep, now is the time to organize them under the proper WARP folders. Any existing or newly created folder is placed as sub folders within the four main categories of the WARP Drive: Work, Admin, Reference and Personal.

Unfortunately you cannot mass move folders in e-mail. So each folder will need to be moved individually.

17. Next, 1Work Sub Folders

Brainstorm your projects. Create separate sub folders for each work project you come up with during your brainstorming. These sub folders are typically specific clients, internal customers, external customers, outputs, and teams you are involved with.

Think core work that you do to create the subfolders. This is a fluid workflow process system that can adapt over time. As new work comes your way, create and name a new subfolder. As work disappears, archive the information if necessary and delete the sub folder.

Everyone's needs are different, but it could look something like this:

Calendar
Contacts
Deleted Items
Inbox
    *Action
    *Follow Up
    *Reading
    1Work
            Clients
            Outputs
            Projects
            Teams
    2Admin
    3Reference
    4Personal
Junk E-mail
Notes
Outbox

18. Next, 2Admın Sub Folders

Create separate sub folders for each admin project you come up with during your brainstorming. These are non-core work activities like filing reports, requests, supervising others, and completing forms.

Admin is work but not core-work. This varies by department. Learning and Development may be admin work for most departments but the core work of the HR or training department. Database processes might be admin for most departments but core work for IT.

Everyone's needs are different, but it could look something like this:

Calendar
Contacts
Deleted Items
Inbox
    *Action
    *Follow Up
    *Reading
    1 Work
    2 Admin
             Expense reports
             Performance appraisals
             Time slips
             Vacation requests
    3 Reference
    4 Personal
Junk E-mail
Notes
Outbox

19. Next, 3Reference Sub Folders

Create separate sub folders for each reference project you come up with during your brainstorming. These are work-related information you will need to consult such as benefits, policies and procedures, artwork and vendors.

Many might confuse admin with reference. Admin involves tasks, while reference is informational. Create folders for information you need to access in the future.

Everyone's needs are different, but it could look something like this:

Calendar
Contacts
Deleted Items
Inbox
    *Action
    *Follow Up
    *Reading
    1 Work
    2 Admin
    3 Reference
        Artwork
        Benefits
        Policies
        Vendors
   4 Personal
Junk E-mail
Notes
Outbox

20. Next, 4Personal Sub Folders

Create separate sub folders for each personal project you come up with during your brainstorming.

Again, subfolders help you find information quicker. So create sub folders that are appropriate to your personal life. For starters, think about categories like: family, friends, education, hobbies, recreation, humor, travel, financial, home, religion or spiritual. No need to get too detailed unless your personal life calls for it.

Everyone's needs are different, but it could look something like this:

Calendar
Contacts
Deleted Items
Inbox
    *Action
    *Follow Up
    *Reading
    1 Work
    2 Admin
    3 Reference
    4 Personal
        Education
        Family
        Friends
        Home
        Travel
Junk E-mail
Notes
Outbox

21. New Project = New Folder

Create a new sub folder when you take on a new project. Don't use your inbox. Remember, *Action or *Follow Up are processing folders, not a catchall for projects.

When is it time to create a new subfolder? Many aspects of your work can be handled in the *Action or *Follow Up folder. You do not need to create a sub folder for every little activity that comes along. However, when it becomes apparent that the activity is going to have an extended life (like a new cross-functional team, organization committee or ongoing project) the time has come to create a subfolder.

22. Advanced: Beyond WARP

For the ultimate in productivity, create WARP folders in the My Documents section of your computer. Use these for saving any attachments and file all e-mails that you want to save for reference.

As an advanced approach we urge all of our productivity coaching clients not to save e-mails within your e-mail program. Instead, store reference e-mails in My Documents on your computer hard drive. E-mail is a communication channel, not a storage facility. So keep the channel clear. Compared to e-mail systems, My Documents is more powerful and simpler to use. Most people find it easier to create, copy, move and store items in My Documents than in MS Outlook.

This does not work for everyone. Some organizations require for legal and security reasons that information stay within the e-mail system. Your IT department should advise you if this is the case.

See section 87 for more on creating WARP in My Documents.

23. No Preview Pane

Set up your e-mail to be read without the preview pane open. Instead of aiding the workflow process, the preview pane slows it down by creating double work.

Reading e-mails in the preview pane is not the same as handling e-mails. Usually it means you have to read the e-mail twice: once in the preview pane and a second time when you open up the e-mail inbox to process.

Caveat: If you do not trust the 'from', viewing an e-mail in preview and not opening it could protect you from virus invasions. This decision should be dependent on the quality of your company's virus protect and spam filtering capabilities.

24. Automatically Open

Set your e-mail program so it automatically opens the next e-mail.

To kill the muda we need to eliminate small wasted steps. There is no one big thing you do to dramatically increase productivity. You make many small incremental improvements, and those little chunks of time each day add up to hours of time savings every week.

This is an example of a small step that will add up to big savings over time. By setting up your e-mail program to automatically open the next e-mail you eliminate the step of individually opening e-mails.

25. From Oldest to Newest

Set your e-mail to be read from oldest to newest.

As you clear out your inbox, read your e-mails from the oldest e-mail to the newest e-mail. As you process the e-mail the next e-mail in chronological order will automatically appear.

What you should not do is skip around processing e-mails and leaving the rest for later. This is a form of muda because it requires twice the effort to process the e-mails.

26. Process With 4 As

Take one of four actions after you read each e-mail: axe, act, allocate, or assign.

Apply the 4 A approach to every e-mail you process. A first decision is whether to take action or not. If not, **Axe** (delete) the e-mail. If yes, then decide which of the remaining three steps to take.

- **Act** means answer within two minutes or less.

- **Allocate** means create time to begin to handle.

- **Assign** means forward it to the person who should be handling.

How you decide to assign can be a thorny question. The following steps offer options for those who are beginners, those who want to take the intermediate course, and the advanced manner for processing. The option is up to you, although we encourage all the people we coach to eventually progress to the advanced way of processing the workflow.

27. Axe It

Axe (delete) every e-mail that you can. Each time you go through your e-mail inbox, if you can delete an e-mail then get rid of it right then.

There is no trick to learning how to delete e-mail. Most of us are quite familiar with the delete key or clicking on the X option in the toolbar. If you are deleting the same types of e-mails over and over again, the real trick may be finding a way to kill the e-mail at the source.

Programs like MS Outlook and Lotus Notes allow you to create rules for the handling of incoming e-mail. Rules act as an administrative assistant. Allow the technology to assist you.

28. Act On It

Act on every e-mail that can be completed in two minutes or less.

Think completion. That is if you can do it swiftly. The objective is not to view an e-mail twice if you don't have to. In fact, many e-mails can be answered in a matter of seconds. Answer or do them and keep the workflow going.

But never sacrifice brevity for clarity. A quick answer is time efficient for you the sender and your receiver, but only if your message is clear. Some people are in the habit of sending a quick message from their Blackberry or iPhone and then send a longer clarifying message when they return to their computer. This often creates double work for you and for the receiver, who has to piece together the two e-mails to get the true picture of what you were trying to communicate. Resist the urge.

29. Allocate It

Allocate the e-mail by moving it forward into your workflow if you cannot complete it in the two minute timeframe.

A secret of increased workflow productivity is making decisions and following through. If this e-mail is something that must be completed today, move it to the *Action folder. If the e-mail requires that you remember to act in the future, move it to Tasks/To Do and you will have entered the request into your to do list. By appending the e-mail you have the information you need to begin the project. By picking a start date you have the peace of mind that this deadline will not sneak up on you and fall between the cracks. Missed deadlines rob productivity from the entire workflow process.

30. Assign It

Assign the e-mail to the responsible / accountable person if is to be completed by someone else.

When the e-mail contains information, or work that is to be accomplished by someone else, immediately forward it to the appropriate person(s). Make sure that you don't become a bottleneck to the completion of work.

Many people that we coach fear "out of sight, out of mind" at this point. After all delegating to someone doesn't relieve you of the responsibility of making sure the work is done. Assigning may require two steps:

- Forwarding to the person doing the work and getting it out of your inbox.
- Tracking for yourself to ensure that the work is done.

This can be accomplished by moving your request from the Sent folder to the *Follow up Folder

31. Move the Value Stream

The purpose of e-mail is to communicate information and work. Driving toward completion of work is always the goal.

Beginner e-mail slayers will use the *Action, *Follow Up, and *Reading to process work. Old e-mail holds reference information.

Intermediate e-mail slayers will use *Action, *Follow Up, and *Reading for processing work and WARP folders to hold reference information.

Advanced e-mail slayers use the 4 As to process the inbox using *Action, *Follow Up, and *Reading for interim parking of short term activities. They use the WARP folders to hold e-mails that are part of dynamic conversations. When those conversations become complete, they either delete the e-mails or move them to My Documents with the "Save As" function as an HTML format.

They use Tasks/To-Dos, Calendars and Contacts to move tasks along the value stream toward completion of the work. (More about that in Part Two).

Which one should you choose? Read on, and start with the approach that feels most comfortable to you. We believe in a crawl, walk, and run approach to creating a workflow productivity process.

32. Check 4 to 6 Times Daily

Decide how many times a day you will check your e-mail. Resist the urge to continuously check e-mails. Checking e-mails four to six times a work day will typically suffice. Reacting to every e-mail is a classic example of muda.

You need to decide that you are the boss of you, not e-mail. You determine how often to check e-mail every day. You allot the necessary amount of time to complete the processing. You commit to processing the entire inbox until empty.

At this point during our seminars and coaching sessions we often get a great deal of push back. People who are used to constantly checking e-mails tell us that this step will never work for them. Their organization is different, their culture demands continuous e-mail checking, or their boss or clients expect nothing less of them. Unless you are a customer service person whose job really demands constant e-mail checking, this is misguided thinking.

We listen patiently. Then we ask them a question: "What happens if someone were sending you something important right now while you are in this seminar? Or on your day off?" The first step to weaning yourself from continuous e-mail checking (and the total loss of concentration that it brings) is making a decision that you can and should do this.

The fact is that if something is that important and urgent, it will not be in your inbox. Remember, you will be emptying your inbox every time you open it. So everything should be current each time. If an issue is that urgent, there will be a phone call or an in-person visit.

33. Empty Inbox Completely

Empty your inbox completely each time you process e-mails. This is crucial to slaying the e-mail monster.

Each time you process e-mails you should completely process every e-mail and not quit until the inbox is empty. You want to be a member of the "Clean Inbox Club".

Many people use their inbox as one giant pending file. Leaving e-mails in your inbox after you read them is counterproductive. Yet it is not uncommon for people to have 50 or more e-mails in their inbox. About 10 percent of people keep 1,000 or more e-mails in the inbox.

Emptying your inbox does not mean completing every item immediately. Instead, it means sorting all the e-mails. The key concept is to process the e-mail workflow, not completely handle every e-mail. Here is the important difference. When you process an e-mail you axe it, act on it, allocate it, or assign it. This is a form of triage, a method of organizing your workflow. Then you can attack the work in an organized, focused manner.

34. Turn Off Ding Thing

Turn off your e-mail alarm and the ghost e-mail preview.

Don't allow features like e-mail alarms and preview panes to constantly distract you. Knowledge work needs focus and concentration.

Most people cannot resist looking at the e-mail when the thing dings. That means stopping what you are doing and switching your mind to a different state. Again, most people just glance at the incoming and close it. Research shows that it takes a full two minutes to get back to concentrating on the work at hand.

If you receive 20 e-mails a day and respond by glancing at it, then getting back to your work, you waste 40 minutes doing nothing but work switching.

35. Specific Subject Lines

Create subject lines for outgoing e-mails that clearly tell the receiver what you are requesting them to do.

Help your e-mail receivers sort, categorize and handle your e-mails by writing very specific subject lines. Try to encourage other members of your team to do the same so you can sort e-mails with greater ease. The best way to do this is to model the behavior to inspire others (this is our version of the E-Mail Golden Rule: e-mail others as you want to be e-mailed).

Here are some examples of specific subject lines:

Subject: Please bring answers to attached questions to staff meeting

Subject: Request permission to reprint your article

Subject: Driving directions to university club for 12/10 meeting

Subject: Request meeting during week of Jan. 12

36. I Love You EOM

If you can communicate your whole message with just a subject line, then do it and add the initials EOM (stands for End of Message) to the end of the subject line.

Sometimes your entire message can be just the subject line. Of course, you will need to be sure your e-mail receivers understand the convention of EOM. Here are some examples:

Subject: Will meet you at 6:30 p EOM

Subject: Bring the TPR report to the meeting 2/10 EOM

Subject: Please send driving directions EOM

Subject: I love you EOM

37. I Love You **NRN**

If you do not need a reply, add the initials NRN (stands for No Reply Necessary) to the end of the subject line.

One way to stop the e-mail smog is to reduce the number of needless replies. Messages like "got it" or "thanks" may seem like the polite thing to do. However it takes time to send these messages and time to read them. With some mutual agreements with the people you exchange e-mails the most with you can greatly reduce these needless replies.

At the end of the subject line add the initials NRN or No Reply Necessary. Here are some examples:

Subject: Please send me your report by 3/10 NRN

Subject: We can discuss the event at the management meeting NRN

Subject: Driving directions are attached NRN

Subject: I will include your comments in the article NRN

38. Reduce FYI E-mail Smog

Don't contribute to e-mail smog by sending general FYI e-mails.

Don't send e-mails because one day you suspect someone on your team may some day have a need for the information in some way. Many busy knowledge workers do not have the time to read and store these long FYI e-mails.

Each e-mail you send should address a specific business situation.

39. One Ask Per E-mail

Stick to one subject per e-mail. Do not load e-mails with multiple requests.

Less is more when it comes to e-mail. A common problem is too many requests within one e-mail. Stick to one subject in your e-mail. Do not include multiple requests in your e-mail. If you have three issues, send three e-mail requests.

This may seem counter-intuitive; however, it increases the clarity of conversation and allows the recipient to respond much quicker.

40. Add Signature Line

Add a signature line to all your e-mails so it is easy for contacts to find you.

Use the auto-signature function on your e-mail program for all outgoing messages. A well-written automatic signature provides important information like who you are and what you do. This also provides information so people can easily get in touch with you by office phone, mobile phone, fax, IM, Facebook, Twitter or even good old fashioned snail mail.

To add a signature, consult the user's guide for your e-mail program and/or check with your IT support desk.

41. Alternate Signature Lines

Create alternate signature files for different types of messages you add to e-mails.

As a real time saver create and use alternate signature files. One example is to add driving directions for people coming to meet you. Your signature for replies could be much less formal. Or you might have a business signature file and then a personal signature file.

42. Acknowledge Complex Requests

When you get a complex request by e-mail, at least notify the sender you have received the e-mail and are working on it. Better yet, give a date when they can expect a reply from you.

Respond by saying "I will get back to you on this by _____ (date)" when you receive e-mails with complex requests. This tells the sender you received their request and are processing it. One benefit of this approach is it reduces the number of follow up e-mails you receive by people checking that you received their previous e-mail.

43. Screen Out Low Value E-mails

Use e-mail program rules to screen out low value recurring e-mails.

Many e-mail programs have rules that you can apply to incoming e-mails. Use the rules feature to either screen out e-mail you don't want or sort the e-mail that you do want.

44. Rules as a Personal Assistant

Use e-mail program to sort routine information and automatically send to your WARP folders

Send certain e-mails you do want to one of your inbox folders. One example is to send e-newsletters you want to route automatically to your *Reading folder. You can read them at your own designated time. Another would be e-mails from family or friends sent to your Personal folder. Folders with new e-mails in them will be bolded and a number in parentheses will show how many are unread.

45. Get Off Lists

Get off e-mail lists you don't want to be on.

If you no longer want to receive e-newsletters or updates that you once signed up for, then get off the list instead of deleting the e-mails each time they arrive. While getting off the list takes a little extra work, it pays off in time savings. If the sender is known, it should be easy to unsubscribe.

Caveat: If it is spam that made it past your company's filter, notify IT and have it added. Trying to unsubscribe personally verifies to the sender that they have your address correct and generates more spam.

46. Choose Proper Channels

Don't send an e-mail when a phone call, face-to-face chat or other communication tool is more appropriate.

For example, do not use e-mail to cancel a meeting that is to occur within 24 hours. Do not assume everyone is checking e-mail continuously (remember, we do not want you to do that either).

According to Lewis Frees, PhD, there are three primary types of communication:

- Handoffs – One way passing of information for use by recipient
- Coordination – Two way communication to get sender & recipient in sync
- Collaboration – Conversations to reach a new understanding or position

Think about the nature of your communication need and then choose the best channel or channel for the job. We suggest this general rule of thumb:

For hand-offs, use anytime channels:

- E-mail
- Snail mail
- Text messaging
- Social media like Linked In, Twitter and Facebook
- E-newsletters

For coordination and collaboration, use same-time channels:

- Telephone
- Face-to-face meetings
- Instant messaging
- PA systems
- Alarms

47. Don't Use E-mail as a Meeting

Avoid multiple and confusing e-mail threads to discuss an issue.

E-mail is good for hand offs but bad for collaboration and complex coordination. We advise against the practice of using e-mail to discuss issues and seek opinions. The problem is these e-mail discussions tend to develop branches of thought.

Too much collective time is spent trying to reconcile the multiple paths the e-mail discussion takes. Instead, of using e-mails in this manner, call a phone meeting or a face-to-face meeting. If participants are spread out, a free telephone bridge line (like www.freeaudioconferencing.com) is an easy way to get everyone on the same phone line.

48. Don't Over Distribute

Resist the urge to hit reply all or attach lists of people to receive copies when it is not necessary.

Reply-to-all is one of the biggest sources of e-mail complaints. When you hit reply-to-all you assume everyone is interested in your response and wants to engage in an ongoing instant conversation about the subject at hand.

But most recipients do not have the time or interest to participate in that kind of conversation. It creates confusion and extra work.

Model the behavior you want other members of your team to adopt. Consider adding a line like the following to your e-mails:

To save time please reply only to me.

49. Train Other People

Train other people on your team or who you communicate with frequently on ways to slay the e-mail monster. You can only do so much on your own to slay the e-mail monster.

Encourage others on your team to send less e-mails. You can start by agreeing to limit the use of Cc: and distribution lists. Just because you *can* send an e-mail to everyone doesn't mean you *should* send an e-mail to everyone.

Copy only those people who truly need to know. Many people feel they are being copied for the wrong reasons. Overuse of Cc: can make the sender seem like they are self-promotional, needy, insecure, manipulative or inefficient. None of these are great for your professional image.

50. Use Out of Office Notification

Use the out of office notification feature on your e-mail when you will be on vacation or personal leave.

Using the out of office notification lowers the sender's expectation about quickly receiving a response. The majority of e-mail senders expect a response within 24 hours. Let technology help you manage expectations.

Tip: Consider using this technique as a "virtual closed door" when you need to create focused concentration time.

51. Delete Previous E-mail Strings

Delete the string of previous e-mails when replying to an e-mail.

When forwarding multiple appended e-mails, either delete the extraneous information or highlight the key points. This will minimize misunderstandings and will save the recipient's time. Let's hope they return the favor.

The worst thing you can do is send a lengthy forwarded train of e-mails with the note to "see below." See what below? You are wasting the sender's time because they have to search for what is important.

By noting the main point of the forwarded e-mail in your opening two sentences you help focus the reader's attention on what is important. By taking just a few seconds to clean up the forwarded e-mail you may save yourself time answering unnecessary return e-mails seeking clarification.

52. Use A-B-C E-mail Formula

Use the A-B-C e-mail formula to write e-mails. A is for the action requested, B is for the background and C is for close.

Stop sending those rambling e-mails. You know the kind. A rambling e-mail takes the indirect approach to reach the point. While reading these vague messages you are ready to rant at your computer, "Get to the point already."

The problem is in our haste to get through the daily onslaught of e-mails we may miss the point. Don't make the readers of your e-mails hunt for the request.

Instead, try this A-B-C formula for writing e-mails. A is for the action you are requesting in the subject line. B is for background, which tells the readers the whys and the wherefores of the request. End with C for close, which is the place for ending with niceties ("thanks for all your hard work") and next steps ("next meeting is 9/15 and we can discuss the rfp process").

53. Clean Folder Club

Join the clean folder club by ending each session and each day with nothing in your inbox. Also delete your junk e-mail folder on a daily basis.

In addition to cleaning your inbox on a daily basis, clean out other parts of your e-mail that may be wasting space. Start with your junk e-mail folder. You might want to do a quick scan to see if anything of value may have accidentally been routed there. At the very least, hit the select all (ctrl A) and then the delete (Del) to send these e-mails to the delete folder.

Next, empty old messages from the delete folder. Another good place to clean up is the Sent folder. The attachments you send can really add up and take up a great deal of storage space. Since you already have these attachments on your computer hard drive this is a form of wasteful, redundant storage of documents.

54. Don't Forward Large Attachments

Think before you forward a large attachment. Some attachments can be quite large and are slow to download.

Ask your IT department and they will tell you that attachments are the figurative bowling ball through the e-mail drainpipe. According to a study by The Radicati Group, e-mail attachments are a major cause of the escalating cost of e-mail for companies. While only about 1 in 5 e-mails contain an attachment, more than 90 percent of corporate e-mail resources are consumed by attachments. The same research noted that the average corporate e-mail user sent and received more than 4MB of daily e-mail attachments.

Ask yourself if you really need to forward that attachment. Most companies have share-drives that are meant for sharing large documents. When a document is ready for distribution, post it on the share-drive and send an e-mail to inform the recipients that it is available for their use.

55. Avoid Multiple Tos

Send an e-mail to only one person when making a request, especially for information. The more people you send an e-mail to means it is less likely any one of them will respond.

If you ask one person for an answer then they are obligated to respond. But if you ask several people for an answer they are apt to think that someone else you wrote to will handle it.

To illustrate, remember the little story about four people named Everybody, Somebody, Anybody, and Nobody.

There was an important job to be done and Everybody was sure that Somebody would do it.

Anybody could have done it, but Nobody did it.

Somebody got angry about that because it was Everybody's job.

Everybody thought that Anybody could do it, but Nobody realized that Everybody wouldn't do it.

It ended up that Everybody blamed Somebody when Nobody did what Anybody could have done

56. Don't Answer Cc

Don't answer e-mails that you were copied on. Especially resist the urge to hit reply all and answer the e-mail.

If you are copied on an e-mail, you are not expected to answer the e-mail. In fact, by answering the e-mail you are adding to the e-mail smog. The worst thing you can do is hit reply all and answer.

This results in multiple people receiving multiple e-mails.

57. Avoid Gossip and Jokes

Don't contribute to e-mail smog by sending gossip and jokes.

Gossip is rumors of a personal, sensational, or intimate nature. These trivial, chatty e-mails are inappropriate and a waste of time for the sender and the receivers.

An e-mail gossip is someone who circulates those incredible e-mails about some celebrity, politician or computer risk. At the very least, you should visit a Web site like www.snopes.com to verify if these messages are in fact true. Here are a few untruths circulating on the Internet:

1. A purported "dry run" by Muslim terrorists on an Air Tran flight.
2. Warning about a computer virus masquerading as a postcard from a friend or family member.
3. E-mailed computer virus masquerades as parcel company's delivery failure notification.
4. Letter by nonagenarian Navy veteran criticizes President Obama.
5. Xerox-sponsored Web sites allows the public to send free postcards to U.S. troops.

6. Warning about cash back charges being surreptitiously placed on Wal-Mart customers' credit cards.
7. Message promises consumers can receive free laptop computers from Ericsson for forwarding an e-mail to their friends.

Circulating jokes, cute pictures and funny headlines may seem like harmless fun, but it is a practice that is adding to the e-mail smog and can potentially have legal risks for the individual and the company. Resist the urge.

58. Reduce After Hours E-mail

Reduce the amount of after hours e-mail that you send. Your actions may be sending the wrong message.

We are not saying to never check or send e-mails after hours, we are just cautioning you to think before you do. One of the reasons is legal. A company that encourages and condones after hour e-mails may be setting itself up for employment law problems.

Managing tech-savvy employees has become the latest compliance challenge under federal and state wage and hour law, according to the national employee law firm Fisher & Phillips LLP. Although litigation regarding this issue is relatively new and the majority of courts have yet to take a definitive position, plaintiffs' lawyers are asserting that even reading or monitoring a BlackBerry or cell phone can amount to compensable time worked. Companies are urged to keep this in mind, along with the unique aspects of your business, when drafting their policies.

A second reason is personal. What image does it send to coworkers when they receive e-mails from you at all hours of the day and night? Is this a person who can't get their work done, or a person who has no personal life?

On the other hand, we understand that, in this global economy, communications across vast time zones are a reality. Using e-mail allows for collaborating in an anytime channel. As with most issues, there is "no one right way".

Part Two.
Groupware Power Trio

Use the groupware power trio of calendar, tasks and contacts to increase your productivity.

Processing e-mail is only half of the battle. Really taking control of your workflow productivity involves being in command of your calendar, your task list and your contacts.

Every knowledge worker is using some form of a calendar, task list and address book. The problems occur when they do not use integrated tools. There is a saying that we use 10 percent of our brains and only 5 percent of the capabilities of our Groupware.

This section will give some tips on how to use your Personal Information Manager (PIM) to move the work farther toward completion. Truly slaying the e-mail monster means relegating it to what it is - just a communication channel. So the work must not stop at the mailbox, it must move beyond. That is where the power trio comes in.

59. Calendar Meetings With You

The most important person to schedule meetings with is you. Schedule the time to work on value activities.

Amid the hustle and bustle of the workday, when are you going to work on the projects that matter? Most people feel guilty scheduling time for themselves. They spend most of their time in react mode; responding to other's demands on their time. How often have you said, "I need to find the time to ….." Well, you can never find the time. You need to *make* the time.

Your job is not processing e-mail and attending meetings. Your job is to produce an output that is part of the value stream of your organization. So, as you recover time from slaying muda, repurpose it to accomplishing work. Schedule small chunks of time dedicated to specific tasks that move your work forward toward completion.

60. Use Calendar As Default

Have calendar + task, not e-mail, as your default window on MS Outlook and similar programs.

Do not have your e-mail screen as your default screen on your computer. This is an invitation to distraction. Even if your computer doesn't make a noise, the new e-mail appearing on your screen is an invitation to stop what you are doing and just take a peek at that new e-mail (who knows, might be more interesting than what you are working on now).

Knowledge work takes focus and concentration. Don't let your concentration be stolen by the next bright, shiny object in your inbox.

61. Only One Calendar

Keep only one calendar. Preferably electronic and make sure it is backed up regularly.

Have you heard the old joke that the person with two watches never really knows what time it is? Something similar can be said about people who keep multiple calendars. These people are never really sure of their schedule.

For knowledge workers we advocate that you merge your professional life calendar with your personal life calendar. There are less chances important appointments and deadlines will fall through the cracks if you use one calendar.

62. If You Must Print

Print the continuously updated PIM calendar if you feel you must have a printed calendar.

We suggest you go digital with your calendar. However, not everyone is comfortable with that. If you must print, use the continuously updated PIM calendar.

PIM is the software for managing contacts, appointments and tasks. It typically includes a name and address contact database, calendar, to-do list task and note taker. PIMs vary widely, but all attempt to provide a convenient way to manage personal information people use on a daily basis.

63. Sync Phone to your Computer

Sync your Blackberry or other PDA to your Computer so you can carry your calendar with you.

Synchronizing your mobile PDA to your PC allows you to install and uninstall applications, transfer files and music, and update and synchronize your Groupware e-mail and calendar. This allows you to take advantage and utilize your PDA to its fullest advantage.

It's called Smartphone for a reason. It's your brains on steroids. Use it!!

64. Sync the Automatic Wireless Way

To further save time, consider syncing your Blackberry or your other PDA to your PC automatically.

To take full advantage of productivity, invest in having your PDA automatically sync to your personal computer or laptop using wireless technology.

With the advance set up this is one chore that can be taken care of automatically. This will ensure that your PDA has the same information as your desktop.

65. Calendar Immediately

Calendar items as soon as you return to your office computer if you do not like adding calendar items on your PDA.

Update your calendar when you return to your desktop computer or laptop after a meeting. This is job number one.

If you wait too long to add the item to your calendar you are in danger of forgetting to add the item or accepting another meeting during that time slot and then contacting one of the parties to reschedule. From a productivity standpoint this is rework, which is one of the worst kinds of muda.

66. Set Meetings
With Calendar, Not E-mail

Use the invite to meeting function that is part of calendar so invitees can easily accept and have the meeting go automatically into their calendar.

Do not trade e-mails to calendar meetings because that adds a step for everyone to get the meeting on their calendar. End the exasperation of e-mail tag trying to set a date and then the wasted step of getting the event on a calendar.

Most e-mail programs have a calendar feature that not only allows you to schedule meetings and due dates, but also sends you reminders. Keep track of dates the convenient way with the calendar feature.

67. Open Your Calendar

Let other people important to you have access to your calendar so they can more easily set meetings with you.

Encourage everyone in your work group to input all meetings and appointments in their electronic calendars. When you do, the calendar search feature can make finding an available meeting time much easier.

You should block out time in your schedule for your value work. By noting this in your calendar you help avoid scheduling conflicts with others who need to meet with you.

68. Recurring Calendar Items

Set up recurring calendar items for regularly scheduled meetings.

Whenever possible use technology to lighten your workload. A great example is using the recurring calendar item feature of your calendar program. This is helpful for recurring staff meetings, training sessions, client meetings, club meetings, classes, and events that happen on a weekly or monthly basis.

When an event is cancelled you can go into your calendar and remove the specific event (like a cancelled class or postponed client meeting). The program gives you the option of canceling all upcoming recurring meetings or just that one time and date.

69. Only One To Do List

Tasks are specific doable activities that can be completed at one sitting. Consider using Tasks in your PIM as your master to do list.

Use the task function of MS Outlook or your similar program to manage your to do list instead of using word processor or spreadsheet programs. Since Tasks are shown on the Calendar, this allows you to see your tasks in context of your day.

We do not recommend immediately prioritizing the 'to do' task list. Some time management experts suggest an A-B-C or 1-2-3 prioritizing system. We think this is wasted effort. Instead manage tasks by categories of work and start dates.

Projects can be broken down into small doable tasks. Each of those tasks can be a separate 'to do' and categorized by the project name. This becomes a good way to manage your projects.

70. Think Start Date not Due Date

Create each task with the same start and end date for every work and personal task you have to do. This ensures that you will be prompted to perform the task.

The most important part of handling a task is picking the day you want to be reminded to do it. In both MS Outlook and Lotus Notes, we recommend making both the start and due dates the same. That way, the task shows on your calendar only on the day you choose to be prompted.

It is possible that you may not be able to perform the task on the day you set. But that is okay. You are still in control. Most PIMs will keep showing the task as overdue so that you won't forget it. You can choose to pick a new time to do the task depending on work load. Or you can use the information to negotiate new deadlines with your client, customer or boss.

71. Keep Adding Tasks

When you think of something new that must be done, add it as a task with the day you will start it.

As you focus on your value work there will always be ideas for new tasks to add. Add them to your task list. You might pick a start date for a time when you expect you might be able to get to this task.

This works in your personal life too. Perhaps it is important to you to clean your garage, but other personal projects are a much higher priority. The task "clean the garage" should still be added to your task list, under the category "personal." Then pick a date when you hope to start that project. As the date approaches a review of your task list will remind you of the job. You can either begin the job or assign a new start date.

One author put it this way: "Remind yourself that Rome wasn't built in a day, but we are building Rome." In other words you can't do it all at once, but you are committed to getting it done.

72. E-mails Trigger Tasks

When an e-mail triggers a task, add it to the task list.

Here is what not to do: don't leave e-mails in your inbox because you want to remind yourself that a request needs to be done. The inbox is not a file cabinet; it is the mailbox to your workspace. But don't stick the request in a folder and forget about it either.

When an e-mail request triggers a task that must be done, create a task and append the e-mail or put the e-mail in the proper folder for when you will need it (the allocate step in the four A process of handling e-mails).

73. Meetings Trigger Tasks

Transfer to do items that come up during meetings from your log to your task list with a start date.

When you return to your desktop PC or laptop after a meeting, enter the tasks that were assigned to you at the meeting. If the meeting was a phone call, try to enter the tasks as soon as you can after you hang up.

Be careful on the days you go from meeting to meeting to meeting (they happen to all of us). A real danger is not recording the requests from the meeting into your task list. This is how many tasks fall into the cracks for an overloaded worker.

74. Planning Triggers Tasks

Transfer to do items that come up during project planning to your task list with a start date.

Remember you are the boss of you. So allocate time to plan your work.

Dashboard planning is the advanced muda killer. You are managing your meetings, your to dos, your self scheduled work, your self generated tasks and your e-mail actions from your groupware.

Now that you are in control of your workflow productivity process, take time to plan your work. Brainstorm what must be done to add value and then schedule the task. This is how you make sure to do what is important, not just what is urgent.

75. Mark Tasks Private

For personal tasks, check the private box so others who have access to your calendar can't see your private tasks.

We advocate the one calendar, one to do list approach so naturally work and personal tasks will be intermingled. Trying to keep multiple systems to separate your work and personal life is counter productive. However, we recommend you keep your private tasks private.

76. Delete Completed Tasks

Delete tasks when you complete them.

If you don't complete a task by its due date, the task will be highlighted in red until you delete it or reassign the start date. By removing completed tasks you make it easier on yourself to focus on tasks that are still pending.

Deleting completed tasks is part of system maintenance and upkeep. Skilled workers know the importance of properly maintaining the tools of their trade. Knowledge workers should be no different.

77. Tasks Should Support Values

Include tasks that support your value work and your personal values.

What is your value work? Constantly ask yourself if you are doing the work that adds value for your clients and your boss. The next step is to add tasks that support your value work.

What about what we call your personal value work? Productivity experts like Franklin-Covey (Dr. Stephen Covey, author of *Seven Habits of Highly Effective People*) advise that you should make sure you include tasks that support your values and strategic goals.

Do you value things like family, faith, spouse, fitness, education, enrichment, recreation, friends and health? Then you need to have tasks that support these or work will fill all available time in your life.

If a task does not support value, delete it. It is just as important to know what *not* to do as to know what to do.

78. Contacts

Use only one address book (contacts).

Hunting for contacts in multiple locations is muda. Consolidate your contacts to one database. Preferably this would be in the Groupware that would live on your computer and be synced wirelessly with your PDA.

Don't save contact information in your e-mail inbox. Moving or copying an e-mail into Address (Contacts) allows for easy capture of sender information.

79. Delegate Contact Inputs

Hire someone else to input your contacts if your time is too valuable to handle this chore.

What do you do if you have contact information in various locations and databases? You need to invest time up front to get your house in order, just like when you had to clean up an overburdened e-mail inbox for the first time (yes we have coached people with more than 1,000 messages they were saving in the inbox).

Investing time to input contacts into your name and address file pays off with time savings down the road when you need to reach people. Hunting for information is wasted efforts that should be eliminated.

Take advantage of technology to speed the process of contact input by using products such as Card Scanner. Or you might hire a temp clerical person to help

80. Include A vCard

Selectively including an electronic business card with your e-mails makes it easy for recipients to add you to their contacts.

Take advantage of e-mail programs that allow you to attach your contact information in the form of an electronic business card. Known as a vCard, with the Internet extension of .vcf, the electronic business card enables the importing of contact information into various e-mail programs.

However you might not want to do this all the time. To deal with the e-mail monster more people are turning to spam filters. Some spam filters are so sensitive they block every e-mail with an attachment and you may not get through to some clients because of the vCard.

81. Use Social Networking

Use social networking Web sites so you can be found.

Put yourself out there on LinkedIn, Plaxo and possibly Facebook so contacts can find you. This is especially crucial if it is important for prospective clients to be able to find you.

82. Add E-mail to Voice-mail

Change your voice-mail greeting to include your e-mail address.

While adding your e-mail address to your voice-mail will increase the number of e-mails you receive, it can reduce time wasted in games of phone tag.

Suppose someone calls you for a piece of information or some assistance and they get your voice-mail message. These people might be calling because they don't know your e-mail address. By adding your e-mail address to your voice-mail message you give them the option of sending the request via e-mail.

83. Add E-mail to Cell Phone

Add your e-mail address to your mobile phone voice-mail too.

Like adding your e-mail address to your voice-mail will increase the number of e-mails you receive, adding your e-mail address to your mobile phone voice-mail will also increase inbound e-mails.

The payoff can be a reduction of time wasted in playing games of phone tag. E-mail is ideal for hand offs because you reach anyone at any time without interrupting them.

Part Three.
Review

It is important to dedicate specific times for "looking at your work."

In manufacturing and other types of work, there are periods of time that are set aside for maintenance of their tools and systems. Many knowledge workers that we have coached have a reluctance to stop the wheel long enough to maintain their own tools and systems.

Reviewing your systems, monitoring your deadlines, coordinating your calendar, etc., are all activities that should be done as part of the normal work cycle. This is what Dr. Stephen Covey calls "Sharpen the Saw".

As Kerry Gleeson states in his _Personal Efficiency Program_, planning is the most important part of any workload management process. So treat this activity as an important part of your work and dedicate work time to it.

84. Daily Review

On a daily basis you should take a few minutes to look over your system. Some people do this at the end of the day for the next day, while others do it as the first chore of the day.

Make sure that the e-mail in your *Action folder has been handled. Remember, it is for things that must be done by the end of the day. Check your *Follow Up to make sure that nothing falls through the cracks. Open your *Reading folder and decide when to read. Don't let these processing folders become procrastination folders.

85. Weekly Review

Set up a recurring weekly meeting with yourself to review the status of your work.

Schedule a 30-minute meeting with yourself to clean up your calendar, tasks, contacts and e-mail folders. This is when you plan your work so you can work your plan for the coming week

During the session, review your *Action, *Follow Up and *Reading folders and then your Task lists. For big projects that you have broken down to small tasks, check to see if you are making the progress necessary or if you need to adjust task start dates.

86. Monthly Review

Set up a recurring monthly meeting with yourself to review tasks for the coming month.

We recommend you schedule a one-hour monthly meeting with yourself for a more detailed planning session. Go through your Task lists to monitor your progress.

At this session look at the following:

- Am I removing muda from my environment?
- Am I standardizing my work flow processes?
- Am I finding time to do the work that is keyed to value?

Remember you work is not handling e-mail. That is only a tool. Your objective should be to focus on the value work that you do. This is the work that your boss and client will hold you accountable for when they review your progress. Kill the muda to buy out the time to spend on this critical work.

Part Four.
Documents

You should have one way of thinking about the information you use in your work. So we suggest that your paper files should mirror your digital files.

The work world is rapidly moving toward a "paper-less" work environment. Most of the paper files we see in our coaching are really printouts of information that was communicated electronically.

There are legitimate reasons for working in hard copy, such as doing detailed scrutiny of large documents. There are also legal reasons for having hard copies of documents with original signatures, such as contracts. The increasing sophistication of digital communication and acceptance of electronic signatures as legal, however, make the case for even less paper.

The paper files that you do have should have the same organization as your electronic files. That way, you have only one way of thinking when looking for information.

87. Create Documents WARP Drive

Create WARP folders in the documents section of your computer. Use the same major headings of Work, Admin, Reference and Personal. You do not need processing folders (*Action, *Follow Up or *Reading).

All stored information should have the same standard framework. Replicate the WARP drive system in your computer's My Documents and your paper filing systems. Using the same organizational scheme will reduce the amount of time spent in retrieving information.

For your personal information, you may want to consider an outside storage device like a USB memory stick (a.k.a flash drive). By using a memory stick you own for your personal information you prevent the data from being stored on your organization's servers.

Your main folders on your computer will be the following:

1 Work
2 Admin
3 Reference
4 Personal*

* You might want to have this on an external USB drive and use a memory stick (a.k.a. flash drive) to store personal information.

88. Create Paper Files

Create folders that live in drawers to manage paper documents.

The business world is moving steadily toward a truly paper-less workspace. In fact, the biggest producers of paper documents are the workers themselves. Keep your desktop clean. Most of the paper piles are self induced. They are comprised of printouts of e-mails, meeting notes, etc.

Then there is reading material. That could be either; something to read and approve, general industry information, trade journals, or other interests.

The desk inbox is no place for piles of this paper and these folders. Begin with action, follow up and reading folders or trays to manage the flow of work as you do with e-mail. The 4 As should be used regardless of the medium that brings the information and work.

The WARP structure can certainly be used as a standard for organizing paper files that are works in progress. Be aware, however, that most documents exist in electronic form. So even if it makes sense to use paper while working on an issue, the completed documentation could be stored electronically.

89. Create Archive Files

Create archive files to be housed out of your workspace.

You do not need immediate access to archived files. This is information you want to keep for legal or historical purposes, but not files you need ready access to.

Good examples of archived files are certain completed projects, legal documents from former customers, and official personnel records. Follow you company's records retention guidelines in deciding which documents can be purged and which must be archived. In either case, these files should not be in your space.

Part Five.
Meetings

Next to e-mail, meetings are often the biggest time wasters in the business world.

To make meetings more productive implement ideas from books like *How to Make Meetings Work*, a classic by Michael Doyle.

Originally published in 1976, Doyle advocates the "Interaction Method" which puts heavy emphasis on the role of a facilitator. Tested on more than 10,000 participants, the Interaction Method of conducting meetings is proven to increase productivity by up to 15 percent.

Doyle says the facilitator's job is to shepherd the meeting to allow for everyone's points of view to be heard, ensure that the meeting progresses towards its stated ends and steps in to assist in resolving conflicts that may arise. Implicit in this role is that the Facilitator does not express his or her opinion regarding any matters that may arise during the course of the meeting.

90. If You Lead, Have An Agenda

Create an agenda if you lead the meeting.

Creating an effective agenda is one of the most important elements for a productive meeting. A good agenda communicates the important topics for discussion, who will be the discussion leader and how much time is allotted for each topic.

A good agenda is also a checklist to ensure that all information is covered. When it is distributed before a meeting, the agenda gives participants a chance to prepare for the meeting discussions and decision making process.

91. Do the Meeting TAP Dance

Use the acronym TAP Dance to remember the elements of a productive meeting: time allocated, agenda, purpose and decisions.

As the meeting leader, you should consider and communicate the following:

- Time. How much time are we allotting for this meeting?
- Agenda. What do we want to cover during the meeting?
- Purpose. What do we want to accomplish?
- Decision. What will be our next step?

92. If You Follow, Suggest An Agenda

Suggest an agenda if you a member of a regularly scheduled meeting that does not use an agenda.

Meeting participants can help the meeting leader in a number of ways. The first is show up on time (think of how much time is wasted in the business world in waiting for someone to arrive for a meeting). A second is to be actively engaged and participating in the meeting.

If there is no agenda a meeting participant can nicely ask TAP Dance questions to guide the process (Time? Agenda? Purpose? Decisions?). Of course, this must be done tactfully.

93. Info, Input or Decision?

Label each agenda item as one of three catego-ries: for information, for input or for a decision. This is helpful for all involved to know what is expected of the group.

Informational items are to inform meeting attendees about the status of a situation. The purpose is to let everyone know what is going on and ask clarifying questions.

Input items are presented by someone who needs to make a decision and requests the views of the attendees. In these cases the decision maker is retaining the power to make the decision, but wants to obtain counsel before making the call.

Decision items are discussions the meeting attendees need to come together and decide. This may be a majority vote or a consensus. This often happens when a committee has been charged with making a decision or a recommendation.

Part Seven.
PDAs

Don't be consumed by PDA addiction.

Personal Digital Assistants (PDAs) like the Blackberry, Treo, Droid, and iPhone are remarkable business tools. These advances in technology offer good news and bad news. The good news is they increase personal productivity by making people available 24/7. The bad news is they increase personal stress by making people available 24/7.

Don't attempt to multitask by constantly checking your PDA whenever and wherever. These productivity devices earned the nickname "Crackberrys" for good reason: people become addicted to constantly checking them. PDAs have become the new business narcotic. The first step to fighting an addiction is to admit you have a problem.

94. Know the Crossword Puzzle Rule

As David Shipley and Will Schwalbe say in their book *Send*, don't take your PDA out unless it would also be socially acceptable to work on a crossword puzzle in the same situation.

If you need to check your Blackberry or iPhone, excuse yourself from the meeting and do it privately.

The truth about PDA dynamics is that workers can be swamped with e-mail all the time, no matter where you are or what you are doing. If this situation really contributed to increased production of value work, it would at least offer some redemption.

The truth is that the promised productivity increase is not being realized. In fact, there is an increasing level of burn out in knowledge workers.

95. Resist Monkey See Monkey Do

Don't play PDA monkey see monkey do.

We advocate modeling the behavior you want others to follow. First is not to bring out your PDA and put it down on the table or desk at a meeting.

But what if the person you are meeting with has taken out their PDA. Just because someone else has taken out their Blackberry (or worse yet, a laptop) at a meeting doesn't mean you should follow suit.

Many people we coach say what they are doing is multitasking. Inevitably a new e-mail pops up and they immediately stop what they are doing to preview it. They say they are multitasking, but the truth is that they are actually work switching. Countless studies show the conscious mind can only deal with one issue at a time. This is a very ineffective way to handle things.

96. Turn Off Pings

Turn off the PDA pings or vibrations that announce to you and everyone else within earshot that you just got mail.

Just like we don't want you constantly distracted at your desk by the audible ping of incoming mail, we don't want you and others distracted by PDA pings as you are out and about. In addition, having the phone on vibrate and resting it on the table creates another distraction for all.

This is not only annoying but shows a lack of attention and respect to others and can result in a loss of social capital.

Final Thoughts

When we began our quest, we started with the premise that the real goal was not to kill the dragon, but to find the princess. It is easy to be so busy fighting monsters, that we forget the real purpose of our jobs. E-mail is only the starting point. Slay muda by eliminating any activities that do not support getting your work done. It is a continuous, disciplined and creative process.

Our mission is helping knowledge workers implement better ways to work – for themselves personally and for their organizations. We've shared with you some of the ways to slay the muda in your e-mail. We ask that you:

1. **Share** *Slay the E-mail Monster* within your organization. We offer substantial discounts for volume sales and/or for bundling with our speaking, workshops and training programs. To learn more, contact us at **951-677-8203.**

2. **Send us your comments**. We'd love to hear your success stories on how you put this information into action. Also send along any thoughts, ideas, articles or books for our future reference. Please e-mail to info@ coffmanvalentine.com.

3. **Visit us online**. Watch our Web site for more ideas and tools on slaying the e-mail monster and killing muda. **Go to www.coffmanvalentine.com.**

References Consulted

These works were helpful to us as we put to paper the work-force process techniques we have taught to our coaching clients at a multitude of organizations.

Allen, David, "*Getting Things Done*", Viking, 2001

Cavanagh, Christina. *Managing Your E-mail: Thinking Outside the Inbox*, John Wiley and Sons, 2003.

Egan, Marsha. *Inbox Detox and the Habit of E-mail Excellence*, Acanthus Publishing, 2009.

Feldman, Susan. "The High Cost of Not Finding Information," KM World, vol. 13, issue 3, 2004.

Gleeson, Kerry "*The Personal Efficiency Program*", John Wiley & Sons, Inc., 2004

Shipley, David and Schwalbe, Will, "*Send*", Alfred A. Knopf, 2008

Song, Mike, Halsey, Vicki and Burress, Tim. *The Hamster Revolution*, Berrett-Koehler Publishers, 2007.

About the Authors

Lynn Coffman and Michael Valentine combined nearly 20 years of independent consulting experience to become partners in the consulting firm of Coffman Valentine & Associates, a company whose consultations focus on individual and workgroup operations.

By combining their differing perspectives and backgrounds, this husband/wife team brings unique insights to its work in individual and group workforce productivity. Lynn's entrepreneurial bottom line and people oriented approach combined with Michael's background in problem solving and business process and structured systems analysis has been instrumental in Coffman Valentine & Associates' successes.

Michael brings the strategic view to the table. Michael has served in executive leadership roles in several corporate and non-profit organizations, with IBM among them. He was also a Director with the Institute for Business Technology (IBT) USA, an arm of IBT International. In his consulting work, Michael works with all levels of personnel from staff to Executives. His focus is driving execution throughout the organization.

Lynn takes a more bottom-up view. Her background in corporate get-it-done project management and relationship building for B-2-B sales underlies her workflow coaching and consultation. She designs methods tailored to the individual or workgroup based on Lean Principles. Her first goal is to help her clients reduce their stress. Then she works collaboratively with her clients to regain control of their work and build skills to increase their productivity.

Acknowledgements

First, and foremost, we would like to thank Henry DeVries, author, consultant and friend, for his sage and practical guidance through the process of creating this, our first book. Henry deserves special recognition for his incredible patience with us for keeping us on track and helping us still stay married. There *are* challenges with working as a husband/wife team!

Thanks goes to all of our clients who made this book possible by allowing us into their work lives. We particularly appreciate the many people at Toyota Motor Sales, U.S.A., Inc. for sharing information to help us better understand Lean Principles so we could help people practically execute and remove waste from all parts of their work.

We want to acknowledge Kerry Gleeson, founder of the Institute for Business Technology International, and the originator of The Personal Efficiency Program. Our association with him over the years has been invaluable. Thanks Kerry!!

Our appreciation also goes to our colleague Dr. Lew Frees for his great insights and willingness to share his extensive research based knowledge and real work execution within his clients.

And special thanks to our friend, Elizabeth Nigro, who bought our first copy of this book even before it was published.

Services Available

Authors Lynn Coffman and Michael Valentine are the founders of Coffman Valentine & Associates (www.coffmanvalentine.com). They provide workflow process productivity training, speaking and consulting. Much of Slay *the E-mail Monster* is based on their entertaining and informative seminars.

Clients range from Fortune 500 corporations to startup entrepreneurial firms, cover all major industry groupings and include both for profit and not-for-profit organizations, including: CareFusion (formerly Cardinal Health), REUTERS, Toyota Motor Sales, U.S.A., Inc., McKee Foods Corp., Toyota Financial Services, Oak Ridge Associated Universities, Guidant Corp, Sempra Energy, American Cancer Society, and Golden State Foods.

Contact Coffman Valentine for more information on how to dramatically increase your team's workflow process productivity.

We can be reached easily by:

Phone:
951.677.8203

E-mail:
lynnc@coffmanvalentine.com
mikev@coffmanvalentine.com